Wellspring

Donna E. Keene

and

Kathy D. Keene

Edited by **Faren Bachelis**   Illustrated by **Jean Franklin**

Prufrock Press, Inc.
P.O. Box 8813
Waco, Texas 76714-8813
(800) 998-2208
Fax (800) 240-0333
http://www.prufrock.com

Table of Contents

*For Christopher,
with thanks to Gary and
our parents*

Introduction

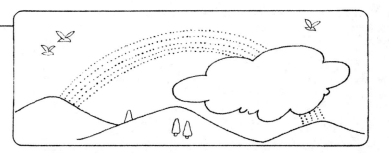

Wellspring is a collection of poetry and creative activities especially selected and developed for gifted children. The material included here will appeal to the abstract thinking, verbal proficiency, love of humor and wide range of knowledge that are characteristic of gifted children in general. Equally important, however, are the suggestions for encouraging each student to make use of his or her own unique talents and interests.

Using poetry as the nucleus, we have developed activities that branch out into other studies such as science, mathematics, music and art. This not only appeals to each child's special area of expertise but helps him or her to see the interrelationship of all fields of knowledge.

Poetry is an ideal subject of study for gifted children. It can encompass as many topics as there are students in the class, for no segment of life is beyond the realm of poetry. Through reading poetry, a student can be in touch with some of the greatest creative minds of all time. Through this book, students will be introduced to such gifted writers as John Keats, Alfred Tennyson, Edgar Allen Poe, Elinor Wylie, Robert Frost and Robert P. Tristram Coffin.

The poems included here express several different philosophies and outlooks. It is very important that gifted children be given the opportunity to consider many points of view. This, in turn, will help them to examine and clarify their own values.

We have approached the study of poetry through the components of rhythm, sound, mood, meaning and humor. The purpose of this book is to instill an appreciation for good poetry and to provide a foundation for further study. This book will not exhaust all aspects of the study of poetry. Rather, it should engender in both teacher and student an abundance of mutually stimulating ideas. Therefore, it is not an end in itself but a beginning—a **Wellspring.**

On Self-Knowledge
Kahlil Gibran

And a man said, Speak to us of Self-Knowledge.

And he answered, saying:

Your hearts know in silence the secrets of the days and the nights.

But your ears thirst for the sound of your heart's knowledge.

You would know in words that which you have always known in thought.

You would touch with your fingers the naked body of your dreams.

And it is well you should.

The hidden well-spring of your soul must needs rise and run murmuring to the sea;

And the treasure of your infinite depths would be revealed to your eyes.

But let there be no scales to weigh your unknown treasure;

And seek not the depths of your knowledge with staff or sounding line.

For self is a sea boundless and measureless.

Say not, "I have found the truth," but rather, "I have found a truth."

Say not, "I have found the path of the soul." Say rather, "I have met the soul walking upon my path."

For the soul walks upon all paths.

The soul walks not upon a line, neither does it grow like a reed.

The soul unfolds itself, like a lotus of countless petals.

Reprinted from *The Prophet*, by Kahlil Gibran, by permission of Alfred A. Knopf, Inc. Copyright 1923 by Kahlil Gibran and renewed 1951 by Administrators C.T.A. of Kahlil Gibran Estate, and Mary G. Gibran.

Chapter 1
The Beat Goes On

Every poem has its own rhythm. In the broadest sense, rhythm means simply a flow or pattern of movement. To illustrate this, it might be helpful to point out that art forms other than poetry have rhythm, too. Music is the most obvious example, but painting, sculpture and architecture can also express movement. Displaying different styles of art, such as Van Gogh's *Starry Night* and a simple line drawing by Picasso, will help to demonstrate this concept.

The poems included in this section illustrate three very different types of rhythm. The excerpt from "The Congo" by Vachel Lindsay brings to mind the primitive beat of tribal revelry and ritual. The rhythm seems to set up a tension between the emotions of excitement and fear. It suggests the measured tempo of jungle drums.

"Sweet and Low" by Alfred Tennyson has a completely different rhythmic pattern. It seems to dispel, rather than build, tension. It has the familiar, comforting rhythm of a lullaby.

The rhythm used by Thomas Hood in "The Song of the Shirt" does not imitate any human or natural movement. Instead, it borrows the abrupt, mechanical pattern that we associate with machines. The rhythm that Hood has chosen serves to reinforce the philosophy expressed in his poem.

After reading these selections, children should be able to recognize how authors employ special rhythm patterns to convey particular meanings and moods.

From **The Congo**

Vachel Lindsay

2. Their Irrepressible High Spirit

Wild crap-shooters with a whoop and a call
Danced the juba in their gambling hall
And laughed fit to kill, and shook the town,
And guyed the policemen and laughed them down
With a boomlay, boomlay, boomlay, BOOM.
THEN I SAW THE CONGO, CREEPING THROUGH THE BLACK,
CUTTING THROUGH THE FOREST WITH A GOLDEN TRACK.
A negro fairyland swung into view,
A minstrel river
Where dreams come true.
The ebony palace soared on high
Through the blossoming trees to the evening sky.
The inlaid porches and casements shone
With gold and ivory and elephant-bone.
And the black crowd laughed till their sides were sore
At the baboon butler in the agate door,
And the well-known tune of the parrot band
That trilled on the bushes of that magic land.

A troupe of skull-faced witch-men came
Through the agate door in suits of flame,
Yea, long tailed coats with a gold-leaf crust
And hats that were covered with diamond-dust.
And the crowd in the court gave a whoop and a call
And danced the juba from wall to wall.
But the witch-men suddenly stilled the throng
With a stern cold glare, and a stern old song:—
"Mumbo Jumbo will hoo-doo you." . . .
Just then from the doorway, as fat as shotes,
Came the cake-walk princes in their long red coats,
Canes with a brilliant lacquer shine,
And tall silk hats that were red as wine.

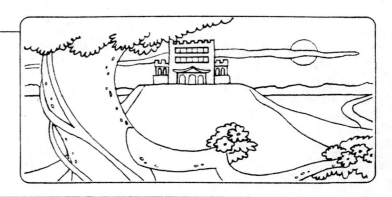

From The Congo

And they pranced with their butterfly partners there,
Coal-black maidens with pearls in their hair,
Knee-skirts trimmed with the jassamine sweet,
And bells on their ankles and little black-feet.
And the couples railed at the chant and the frown
Of the witch-men lean, and laughed them down.
(Oh, rare was the revel, and well worth while
That made those glowering witch-men smile.)

The cake-walk royalty then began
To walk for a cake that was tall as a man
To the tune of "boomlay, boomlay, BOOM,"
While the witch-men laughed, with a sinister air,
And sang with the scalawags prancing there:—
"Walk with care, walk with care,
Or Mumbo-Jumbo, God of the Congo,
And all the other Gods of the Congo,
Mumbo-Jumbo will hoo-doo you.
Beware, beware, walk with care,
Boomlay, boomlay, boomlay, boom.
Boomlay, boomlay, boomlay, boom.
Boomlay, boomlay, boomlay, boom.
Boomlay, boomlay, boomlay
BOOM."
(Oh, rare was the revel, and well worth while
That made those glowering witch-men smile.)

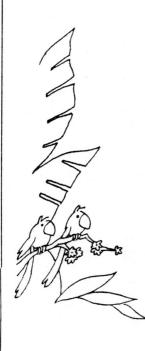

9

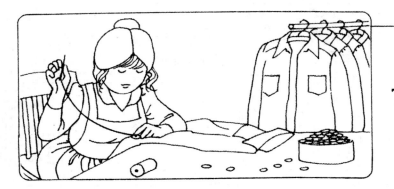

The Song of the Shirt (Abridged)

Thomas Hood

With fingers weary and worn,
  With eyelids heavy and red,
A woman sat, in unwomanly rags,
  Plying her needle and thread—
Stitch! stitch! stitch!
  In poverty, hunger, and dirt,
And still with a voice of dolorous pitch
  She sang the "Song of the Shirt."

"Work—work—work,
  Till the brain begins to swim;
Work—work—work—
  Till the eyes are heavy and dim!
Seam, and gusset, and band,
  Band, and gusset, and seam,
Till over the buttons I fall asleep,
  And sew them on in a dream!

"Oh, men, with sisters dear!
  Oh, men, with mothers and wives!
It is not linen you're wearing out
  But human creatures' lives!
Stitch—stitch—stitch,
  In poverty, hunger, and dirt,
Sewing at once, with a double thread
  A Shroud as well as a Shirt.

"But why do I talk of Death?
  That phantom of grisly bone,
I hardly fear its terrible shape,
  It seems so like my own—
It seems so like my own,
  Because of the fasts I keep;
Oh, God! that bread should be so dear,
  And flesh and blood so cheap!

"Work—work—work!
  My labor never flags;
And what are its wages? A bed of straw,
  A crust of bread—and rags.
That shattered roof—this naked floor—
  A table—a broken chair—
And a wall so blank, my shadow I thank
  For sometimes falling there!

"Work—work—work!
  From weary chime to chime,
Work—work—work,
  As prisoners work for crime!
Band, and gusset, and seam,
  Seam, and gusset, and band,
Till the heart is sick, and the brain benumbed,
  As well as the weary hand.

Seam, and gusset, and band,
  Band, and gusset, and seam,
Work—work—work,
  Like the engine that works by steam!
A mere machine of iron and wood
  That toils for Mammon's sake,
Without a brain to ponder and craze
  Or a heart to feel—and break!

With fingers weary and worn,
  With eyelids heavy and red,
A woman sat, in unwomanly rags,
  Plying her needle and thread—
Stitch! stitch! stitch!
  In poverty, hunger, and dirt,
And still with a voice of dolorous pitch—
Would that its tone could reach the rich!—
  She sang this "Song of the Shirt!"

Song

Alfred Tennyson

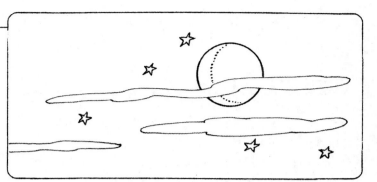

Sweet and low, sweet and low
   Wind of the western sea
Low, low, breathe and blow,
   Wind of the western sea!
Over the rolling waters go,
Come from the dying moon, and blow,
   Blow him again to me;
While my little one, while my pretty one, sleeps.

Sleep and rest, sleep and rest,
   Father will come to thee soon;
Rest, rest, on mother's breast,
   Father will come to thee soon;
Father will come to his babe in the nest,
Silver sails all out of the west
   Under the silver moon:
Sleep, my little one, sleep, my pretty one, sleep.

The Congo — *Discussion Questions*

1. What is a cake walk?

2. What type of dance is the juba and where did it originate?

3. Who were the witch-men and what control did they have over the people?

4. The witch-men told the people to "walk with care." What was meant by this?

5. How did the witch-men react to the revelry?

6. Throughout the poem Lindsay repeats the phrase "boomlay boom." What does this sound remind you of?

7. What does Lindsay mean by "Then I saw the Congo, creeping through the black"?

8. America is comprised of many different ethnic groups. Do any of your families retain customs from the country of their origin? Share them with the class.

9. How has the mixing of cultures shaped the character of America? What details in this poem illustrate the mixing of cultures?

The Song of the Shirt — *Discussion Questions*

1. What does the rhythm of this poem remind you of?

2. Find out when this poem was written. What were conditions like for the working class at this time?

3. What is a shroud?

4. The woman in the poem was "Sewing at once, with a double thread,/A Shroud as well as a Shirt." In what way could she be doing both at once? Who is the shroud for?

5. What inanimate thing does the poet compare the worker to? In what ways are they alike?

6. Have you ever worked on something that required you to keep repeating the same motions over and over again? How did it make you feel?

7. Have you ever heard the word "dehumanized"? What does it mean?

8. How can a human being be "dehumanized"? Have you ever felt that way? Explain.

9. What kinds of wages is the woman receiving for her work? What is it costing her?

10. How does the rhythm of this poem compare with that of "The Congo"?

11. The poet breaks the usual rhythm of the poem in the last stanza by adding an extra next-to-last line. Why do you think he does this? What is the effect?

12. Think of occupations existing today that endanger the health of workers. Explain how. Can any of these be remedied? How?

13. Can repetitive work ever be pleasant? What other conditions would be necessary to make it so? Explain.

Song — *Discussion Questions*

1. Which words are repeated most often?

2. Where do you think the father mentioned in the poem is?

3. What is the definition of the word lullaby? Where did it originate?

4. What restful motions are mentioned in this poem?

5. What things does the rhythm of the poem make you think of?

6. What characteristics do lullabies have in common?

7. Do you remember lullabies your mother sang? Why did they appeal to you?

The Beat Goes On — *Activities*

The Congo

1. Children will be able to understand the concept of rhythm more quickly by reproducing or creating their own rhythmic patterns.

   One way in which children can physically feel rhythm is by bouncing balls to musical selections. The beat should be fairly consistent. A good one to start with might be the *Grand Canyon Suite*. Gradually have children move on to more complicated rhythm patterns.

   Suggest to the children that different rhythm patterns can be created by using objects available to them at their desks. This could include pencil tapping, foot stomping, finger snapping and all the other activities that teachers usually try to discourage!

2. "The Congo" presents an irresistible rhythm pattern. Students should read the poem out loud, using drums, tambourines and triangles to highlight the rhythm. Have some members of the class create a jungle mural to be used as a backdrop for a choral presentation. Others could work on smiling and frowning witch-men masks and costumes.

3. "The Congo" makes reference to diamonds, gold and ivory—all natural resources of Africa. Have students research the exploration and/or exploitation associated with these natural resources.

4. Arrange a visit from a leader of a local ethnic organization to discuss the importance of preserving cultural traditions.

5. Collect traditional musical selections from different countries and play them for the students. Ask the children to identify from which country or part of the world the music originated. Discuss which selections students enjoyed most and why.

The Beat Goes On — *Activities*

Song

1. The poem by Alfred Tennyson has a completely different rhythm from that of "The Congo." After the children have read the poem, ask what the rhythm suggests to them. Possible responses might be the ebb and flow of the sea, the rising and dying of the wind or the rocking of a cradle.

   Encourage discussion of why each poem employs its particular rhythm, keeping in mind the purpose of the author in each case. If Tennyson had used the same type of rhythm as Lindsay, what would the effect have been?

2. Tennyson's poem has been set to music. Perhaps your music teacher could have the children sing it as a lullaby.

3. Have students research lullabies from various countries and report to the class. Do they notice similarities in the rhythm of the lullabies? Are there cultural differences apparent in the messages conveyed by the songs?

The Beat Goes On — *Activities*

The Song of the Shirt

1. Have students read aloud passages from "The Song of the Shirt" while others portray the women mechanically stitching shirts. Have the class decide on appropriate props and an effective ending for the dramatization. Some members of the class could write their own dialogue for a separate skit to show how these women might have felt about their lives.

2. Many occupations today require workers to repeat movements in a mechanical fashion. Have the students discuss what forms of employment in their town or surrounding area could be characterized in this way.

   If possible, set up a field trip through several of these plants. Have each student choose one of the jobs discussed and write a short verse that gives a feeling for the work through the rhythm and words used. Ask that they illustrate their poems with an original drawing, painting or collage.

3. Instruct students to find out about practices of the garment industry today. How are working conditions today different from those of Victorian England? What laws and union rules protect the workers? Are there any dangerous conditions or practices remaining that should be changed? Have the students present their findings through the setting of an investigative reporter interviewing workers and union leaders.

The Beat Goes On — *Activities*

General Activities

1. If the children seem interested in the previous activities, they might enjoy putting various rhythms together for a stage production. You might select a theme such as "Rhythm at Work," in which children portray people doing various jobs, each creating his or her own rhythmic pattern.

   Occupations might include a secretary typing, a construction worker hammering, a carpenter sawing wood, a tap dancer performing and a homemaker perking coffee. Less obvious characters might include a farmer milking a cow (sound effects supplied by squirting water pistols into a pail), a politician droning on, supplying a background rhythm, or a singer practicing the scale. Your music teacher could help coordinate the various rhythms to make a symphony of sounds. Students will no doubt think of their own personal touches, such as costumes, backdrop and lighting, to enhance the production. They might wish to conclude the production with some special sound effect such as a lunch whistle blowing or the click of a light being switched off.

14

Chapter 2
It's a Beautiful Sound!

The poet uses sounds to convey a mood, to establish a certain rhythm or to define a situation.

Poe uses the sounds of different types of bells to convey the human emotions of merriment, happiness, terror and sorrow. Throughout the poem the selection of words and changes in tempo create different moods.

For example, "jingling" and "tingling" suggest the light, festive sound of sleigh bells, while "clang" and "twang" describe the discordant sound of the alarm bell. Such words imitate actual sounds; this device is known as onomatopoeia.

In Elinor Wylie's poem, the words do not imitate sounds, but are sounds. "Pretty Words" describes some of the poet's favorites by comparing them to animals. For example, the phrase, "gold-enameled fish," exemplifies the smooth-sounding words she likes. All the animals she mentions are rather docile, like the "pet words" she describes.

In "Lone Dog," Irene McLeod describes one animal, a fiercely independent dog. The words she uses are rough and wild like the dog itself. She uses many hard consonant sounds to give us a feeling of the harsh life this dog leads.

15

The Bells

Edgar Allen Poe

Hear the sledges with the bells—
Silver bells!
What a world of merriment their melody fortells!
How they tinkle, tinkle,
In the icy air of night
While the stars that oversprinkle
All the heavens seem to twinkle
With a crystalline delight;
Keeping time, time, time
In a sort of Runic rhyme,
To the tintinnabulation that so musically wells
From the bells, bells, bells, bells,
Bells, bells, bells—
From the jingling and the tinkling of the bells.

Hear the mellow wedding bells,
Golden bells!
What a world of happiness their harmony foretells!
Through the balmy air of night
How they ring out their delight!
From the molten-golden notes,
And all in tune,
What a liquid ditty floats
To the turtle-dove that listens, while she gloats
On the moon!
Oh, from out the sounding cells
What a gush of euphony voluminously wells!
How is swells!
How it dwells
On the future! how it tells
Of the rapture that impels
To the swinging and the ringing
Of the bells, bells, bells
Of the bells, bells, bells, bells,
Bells, bells, bells—
To the rhyming and the chiming of the bells!

Hear the alarm bells—
Brazen bells!
What a tale of terror, now their turbulency tells!
In the startled ear of night
How they scream out their affright!
Too much horrified to speak,
They can only shriek, shriek
Out of tune,
In a clamorous appealing to the mercy of the fire,
In a mad expostulation with the deaf and frantic fire,
Leaping higher, higher, higher,
With a desperate desire

And a resolute endeavor
Now—now to sit, or never
By the side of the pale faced moon.
Oh, the bells, bells, bells!
What a tale their terror tells
Of despair!
How they clang, and clash, and roar!
What a horror they outpour
On the bosom of the palpitating air!
Yet the ear it fully knows,
By the twanging,
And the clanging,
How the danger ebbs and flows;
Yet the ear distinctly tells,
In the jangling,
And the wrangling,
How the danger sinks and swells,
By the sinking or the swelling in the anger of the bells—
Of the bells—
Of the bells, bells, bells, bells,
Bells, bells, bells—
In the clamor and the clangor of the bells!

Hear the tolling of the bells—
Iron bells!
What a world of solemn thought their melody compels!
In the silence of the night,
How we shiver with affright
At the melancholy menace of their tone!
For every sound that floats
From the rust within their throats
Is a groan.
And the people—ah, the people—
They that dwell up in the steeple,
All alone,
And who tolling, tolling, tolling,
In that muffled monotone,
Feel a glory in so rolling
On the human heart a stone—
They are neither man nor woman—
They are neither brute nor human—
They are Ghouls:
And their king it is who tolls;
And he rolls, rolls, rolls,
Rolls
A paean of the bells!
And his merry bosom swells
With the paean from the bells!
And he dances and he yells;
Keeping time, time, time,
In a sort of Runic rhyme,
To the throbbing of the bells—
Of the bells, bells, bells—
To the sobbing of the bells;
Keeping time, time, time,
As he knells, knells, knells,
In a happy Runic rhyme,
To the rolling of the bells—
Of the bells, bells, bells—
To the tolling of the bells,
Of the bells, bells, bells, bells—
Bells, bells, bells—
To the moaning and the groaning of the bells.

17

Pretty Words

Elinor Wylie

Poets make pets of pretty, docile words:
I love smooth words, like gold-enameled fish
Which circle slowly with a silken swish,
And tender ones, like downy-feathered birds:
Words shy and dappled, deep-eyed deer in herds,
Come to my hands, and playful if I wish,
Or purring softly at a silver dish,
Blue Persian kittens, fed on cream and curds.

I love bright words, words up and singing early;
Words that are luminous in the dark, and sing;
Warm lazy words, white cattle under trees;
I love words opalescent, cool and pearly,
Like midsummer moths, and honied words like bees,
Gilded and sticky, with a little sting.

Lone Dog

Irene Rutherford McLeod

I'm a lean dog, a keen dog, a wild dog, and lone;
I'm a rough dog, a tough dog, hunting on my own;
I'm a bad dog, a mad dog, teasing silly sheep;
I love to sit and bay the moon, to keep fat souls from sleep.

I'll never be a lap dog, licking dirty feet,
A sleek dog, a meek dog, cringing for my meat,
Not for me the fireside, the well-filled plate,
But shut door, and sharp tone, and cuff and kick and hate.

Not for me the other dogs, running by my side,
Some have run a short while, but none of them would bide.
O mine is still the lone trail, the hard trail, the best,
Wide wind, the wild stars, and hunger of the quest!

Reprinted with permission of the Author's Literary Estate and Chatto & Windus Ltd., from *Songs to Save a Soul*, by Irene Rutherford McLeod.

The Bells — *Discussion Questions*

1. What does the word "tintinabulation" mean?

2. What does "runic rhyme" mean?

3. Which bells does the poet seem to enjoy the most? What sound words does he use to describe them?

4. Which bells does he dislike the most? Why do you think he feels this way?

5. What does the tolling of the iron bells signify?

6. What institution does Poe associate with the iron bells?

7. Who do you think are the people who dwell up in the steeple?

8. In the final stanzas Poe directs his anger at the bells and some imaginary creatures he calls ghouls. Is this what he is really angry at? Explain.

Pretty Words — *Discussion Questions*

1. What does the word "docile" mean?

2. If you were to rename the poem "Pretty Words" what would you call it?

3. What is alliteration? Can you find examples of this in the poem?

4. What animal does Elinor Wylie refer to that is not as docile as the others? Why might she have included that one?

5. How could words be considered pets?

6. Have you ever heard the word pet used to describe something other than an animal? List as many ways as you can. How do you think these phrases developed?

7. Are there words whose sound is offensive to you? Can you separate the sound of a word from its meaning?

Lone Dog — *Discussion Questions*

1. The speaker in the poem "Lone Dog" uses many harsh words to describe himself and the life he leads. How do you think the author feels about the dog?

2. What indications are there in the poem that the "Lone Dog" might be a little envious of the more pampered dogs mentioned in the poem? Have you ever made fun of something you really wanted to have? Explain.

3. Do you think the dog has been abused? Why?

4. Is the dog satisfied with his life?

5. Can you think of characters from literature or television that are like the "Lone Dog"?

6. What might the quest mentioned in the final line have been? Do you think the dog knew?

7. Have you ever felt the urge to get away from familiar people and places? Did you have a clear idea of where you wanted to go and what you wanted to do? Explain.

It's a Beautiful Sound! — *Activities*

The Bells

1. For this activity, provide a string of jingle bells, an alarm clock with a bell top, two chiming bells of different tones and a copper-bottomed pan and a wooden spoon (to represent the tolling of a church bell). Let the children examine these materials to hear the sound each makes.

   Ask the students to read the sections of Poe's poem that describe different kinds of bells. Have them choose the instrument that best represents the sound of each bell. Then let them read "The Bells" using these sound effects to highlight the poem.

   Discuss the sound words that Poe uses, such as "tinkle," "twanging," "tolling," etc. Ask how the words he uses tell us what type of bell he is describing.

2. Have the more science-minded students in your class experiment with the pitch and tone of bells by making some of their own. Very basic bells could be made by using various size clay pots and different size clangers.

3. Investigate the origin of bells or the various uses of bells as found in the home, in business, in entertainment or for religious purposes.

It's a Beautiful Sound! — *Activities*

Pretty Words

1. Ask the children whether they have any "pet" words they especially like. They might be "pretty, docile words" or "rough" and "tough" ones. Have them explain why they like their chosen words.

2. Find at least eight types of words that Elinor Wylie describes in her poem, such as "smooth words" and "bright words." Set them up as category headings on a chart. Choose some of your own favorite words that fit under each heading. Add to the list as you read more poems.

It's a Beautiful Sound! — *Activities*

Lone Dog

1. The chapter entitled "The Cat," from *The Summer Book* by Tove Jansson,[1] describes how a girl traded her independent, unaffectionate pet for one that was tame and complacent. Surprisingly, she was not as happy with her decision as she thought she would be. The children might like to read the chapter and discuss what happened.

   [1] Tove Jansson, *The Summer Book*, Pantheon Books.

It's a Beautiful Sound! — *Activities*

General Activities

1. "Pretty Words" and "Lone Dog" use words effectively to create completely different feelings. Read words and phrases from "Pretty Words" and ask students to find words and phrases from "Lone Dog" that either are opposite in meaning or convey a completely different atmosphere. Examples and suggested responses are included here. Discuss any words that might be unfamiliar.

"Pretty Words"	"Lone Dog"
docile	wild
smooth	rough
tender	tough
playful	mad
purring softly at a silver dish	sit and bay the moon
up and singing early	hunting on my own
fed on cream and curds	shut door. . . cuff and kick and hate
warm lazy	lone trail. . . hard trail

2. Ask children to choose which animals in the poems they would like to have as pets and explain why. They could then discuss what qualities make a good pet. Would any of them like to have a dog like the one described in Irene McLeod's poem? Are there people they know that remind them of that dog? Do pets sometimes act like their owners?

3. Have the children go through the school recording different sounds they hear, such as the typewriter in the office, bells ringing, trays being moved about in the cafeteria and various sounds on the playground. Have them play the tape for other members of the class who will try to identify each sound. Let them write a word for each sound they hear and suggest that they incorporate some of these sound words in a poem.

4. Have the children look through *The Lorax,* by Dr. Seuss,[2] and find some made-up words. They will find such words as "glumping," "gluppity-glupp," "smogulous," "snuvv" and many more. Even though these are made-up words, the meaning is clear from the context, the sound of the word and the fragments of other words each contains.

   Children have probably heard younger brothers and sisters substitute a made-up word for a real word. "Squishion" is a child's made-up word. Can you guess what a "squishion" might be? The child has combined two words, cushion and a word that describes its physical quality, squishy.

   Have the children divide into two groups. Have one group write descriptions of new inventions and products. Have the other group give these products and inventions original names. The names might consist of real or made-up words.

5. Have the students list five sounds they find pleasing and five that are irritating to them. Ask them to make up a word that imitates each of those sounds. An example might be the cry of a baby represented by the word "waaugh," or the falling rain represented by "plip plop." Have them read and compare their lists in class. How did likes and dislikes compare?

6. Have each student write a short description of a scene. Collect papers and redistribute them so each student has a scene other than his or her own. Then have students decide what sound effects would be appropriate for each scene and how they might be produced. Have a variety of materials available, such as wooden spoons, school instruments, sandpaper, bottles, etc. Have each student produce his or her scene with sound effects for the class.

[2]Dr. Suess, *The Lorax,* Random House.

Chapter 3
Figuratively Speaking

Some poems describe a scene or an experience; others tell a story or entertain. Often poets have a special meaning they wish to convey. They may use figures of speech to point out a new or unusual way of viewing something.

"The Spider," is packed with images. They can be looked at as puzzles to be solved in order to find the author's meaning. If the title were not given, the whole poem might be considered a riddle. The word "spider" is never used, but that little animal and his world are described in detail through various metaphors and similes.

"Song," by John Keats, contains no figures of speech, yet the poem has a meaning beyond the simple story of the death of a bird. The poet uses this example to symbolize a larger problem of life—the danger of loving for selfish reasons.

"A Dream Deferred" contains a number of powerful similes and concludes with a single metaphor. The author has skillfully used figures of speech to illustrate a range of human emotions. "A Dream Deferred" takes on an even greater significance when we learn that its author, Langston Hughes, was a black man.

The section concludes with a group of three short poems that use similes and metaphors to describe the moon and its qualities. Two of Vachel Lindsay's poems are included here. The first compares the moon to a cooky and seems to be written from a child's point of view. The speaker offers a unique explanation of the phases of the moon.

In Lindsay's poem "The Old Horse in the City," the moon is seen as a basket of corn by the tired and abused old horse. The moon embodies the horse's longing for a better life.

In Christopher Morley's poem, the moon is compared to a docile sheep that sometimes wanders beyond her normal boundaries. When she finally returns to her usual surroundings of the night, she is reunited with her lambs, the stars.

The Spider

Robert P. Tristram Coffin

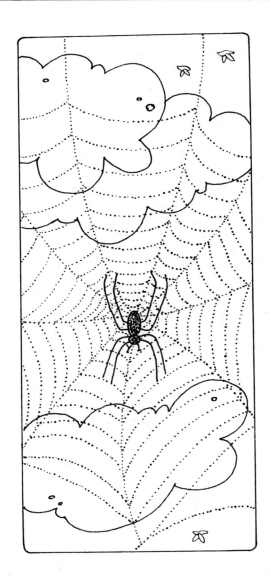

With six small diamonds for his eyes
He walks upon the Summer skies,
Drawing from his silken blouse
The lacework of his dwelling house.

He lays his staircase as he goes
Under his eight thoughtful toes
And grows with the concentric flower
Of his shadowless, thin bower.

His back legs are a pair of hands,
They can spindle out the strands
Of a thread that is so small
It stops the sunlight not at all.

He spins himself to threads of dew
Which will harden soon into
Lines that cut like slender knives
Across the insects' airy lives.

He makes no motion but is right,
He spreads out his appetite
Into a network, twist on twist,
This little ancient scientist.

He does not know he is unkind,
He has a jewel for a mind
And logic deadly as dry bone
This small son of Euclid's own.

Dream Deferred

Langston Hughes

What happens to a dream deferred?

Does it dry up
like a raisin in the sun?
Or fester like a sore—
And then run?
Does it stink like rotten meat?
Or crust and sugar over—
like syrupy sweet?

Maybe it just sags
like a heavy load.

Or does it explode?

Song

John Keats

I had a dove and the sweet dove died;
    And I have thought it died of grieving:
O, what could it grieve for? it was tied
    With a silken thread of my own hand's weaving;
Sweet little red feet! why did you die—
    Why would you leave me, sweet dove! why?
You liv'd alone in the forest-tree,
    Why, pretty thing! could you not live with me?
I kiss'd you oft and gave you white peas;
    Why not live sweetly, as in the green trees?

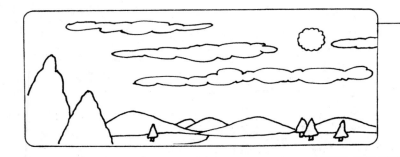

The Moon-Sheep

Christopher Morley[1]

The moon seems like a docile sheep,
She pastures while all people sleep;
But sometimes, when she goes astray,
She wanders all alone by day.

Up in the clear blue morning air
We are surprised to see her there,
Grazing in her woolly white,
Waiting the return of night.

When dusk lets down the meadow bars
She greets again her lambs, the start!

The Moon's The North Wind's Cooky

Vachel Lindsay[2]

The Moon's the North Wind's cooky
He bites it day by day,
Until there's but a rim of scraps
That crumble all away.

The South Wind is a baker.
He kneads clouds in his den,
And bakes a crisp new moon that . . . greedy
North . . . Wind . . . eats . . . again!

[1] "The Moon-Sheep" from *Chimneysmoke* by Christopher Morley, (J.B. Lippincott, Publishers). Copyright, 1917, 1945 by Christopher Morley. Reprinted by permission of Harper & Row, Publishers, Inc.
[2] Reprinted with permission of Macmillan Publishing Co., Inc. from *Collected Poems* by Vachel Lindsay. Copyright 1914 by Macmillan Publishing Co., Inc., renewed 1942 by Elizabeth C. Lindsay.

The Old Horse in the City

Vachel Lindsay

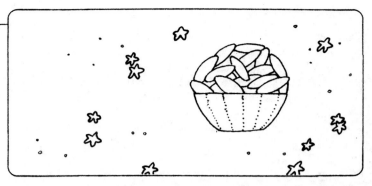

The moon's a peck of corn. It lies
Heaped up for me to eat.
I wish that I might climb the path
And taste that supper sweet.

Men feed me straw and scanty grain
And beat me till I'm sore.
Some day I'll break the halter-rope
And smash the stable-door,

Run down the street and mount the hill
Just as the corn appears.
I've seen it rise at certain times
For years and years and years.

New York: Macmillan Publishing Co., Inc., 1913.

© Prufrock Press Inc.—*Wellspring*

The Spider — *Discussion Questions*

1. Why does the author say the spider has "six small diamonds for his eyes"?

2. How can a spider "walk upon the summer skies"?

3. What is unique about the building materials that the spider uses?

4. How does the spider lay "his staircase as he goes"?

5. What does the word "concentric" mean?

6. What is the "concentric flower" mentioned in line 7?

7. Why are the spider's back legs called "a pair of hands"?

8. How do the spider's lines "cut. . . across the insects' airy lives"?

9. Why does Coffin say the spider "spreads out his appetite into a network"?

10. Who was Euclid? Why is the spider described as Euclid's son?

11. How do you think the author feels toward spiders? Pick out a line from the poem that would support your idea.

12. What is the mood of this poem? What words has the author chosen to create this mood?

13. Name some words that could have been used to describe a spider or his home that would have created a completely different mood.

14. Did this poem make you feel or think any differently about spiders than you did before? How?

Song — *Discussion Questions*

1. What does "grieving" mean?

2. What did the speaker think had made the dove die?

3. Do you think he was right in thinking this? Explain.

4. How had he treated the dove? What specific things had he done to take care of it?

5. Do you think the "silken thread" might symbolize anything else? Explain.

6. Why was the speaker surprised and puzzled at the death of his pet?

7. Had he really cared about the bird? Give reasons for your opinion.

8. How old do you think the speaker in the poem might be? Describe what he or she might be like.

9. What had the owner failed to give his pet that was necessary for the bird's survival?

10. Can love be selfish? Explain how or how not.

Dream Deferred — *Discussion Questions*

1. What does the word "deferred" mean?

2. Have you ever had a dream deferred? How did it make you feel?

3. Find the similes in the poem and underline them.

4. How can an unfulfilled dream be like each of the situations described by the similes? What different emotions or behaviors would be involved? Discuss with the class.

5. In what different ways do people react to disappointment?

6. Why did Hughes conclude the poem as he did? How is the final figure of speech different from the others?

7. Have you ever "exploded" when things you'd planned did not turn out the way you wanted them to? Explain.

8. Is there a good way to get rid of angry feelings and frustrations? Explain.

9. Do you think the poet might have gotten rid of any anger or frustration through writing this poem? Explain.

10. Briefly research the life of Langston Hughes. What circumstances in his life might have nurtured the feelings expressed in this poem?

The Moon's The North Wind's Cooky — *Discussion Questions*

1. How does the moon look like a cooky?

2. What characteristics of the moon is the poet describing in lines 2-4?

3. What does the "rim of scraps" refer to?

4. What is he comparing the clouds to?

5. Why is the South Wind the baker and the North Wind the consumer?

The Moon-Sheep — *Discussion Questions*

1. What characteristics would the moon and a sheep have in common?

2. Why would they both be called docile?

3. What does the poet mean by the line, "She pastures while all people sleep"?

4. How does the moon go "astray"?

5. How could the stars be considered the moon's lambs?

The Old Horse in the City — *Discussion Questions*

1. Who is the speaker in the poem?

2. What does the horse say the moon is?

3. How will the horse reach his destination?

4. Does the speaker really think the moon is corn?

5. How has the horse been treated?

6. What is meant by "asking for the moon"? Can you think of other sayings that mention the moon?

Figuratively Speaking — *Activities*

The Spider

1. Spiderwebs are ingenious traps as well as breathtaking works of art. Students wishing to learn more about this subject will enjoy the transcript of the *Nova* program, "Life on a Silken Thread,"[1] a fascinating study of spiders and their world.

2. Spiderwebs may be collected and mounted permanently. First, spray the web while it is still in place with colored lacquer. Stand far enough away so the web will not be damaged. Use several coats of very fine mist. When the web is the desired color, position a piece of paper behind it and carefully bring the paper up against the web. Carefully cut the strands off at the edge of the paper. Spray with a fixative to make it more durable. Caution children to be extremely careful with fixatives.

3. Students interested in math or geometry could examine photographs or actual webs to see how many geometric shapes and types of angles they can identify.

Figuratively Speaking — *Activities*

Song and The Old Horse in the City

1. Contact someone from the Humane Society who might speak to the class about the care of animals. How do even well-meaning people cause suffering to animals? What are the most common abuses?

2. Help students arrange an interview with a member of the forestry department or an official of the Environmental Protection Agency to learn about how the human impact on the ecology has affected local wildlife. Are any species in the area in danger of extinction? If so, what is being done to prevent that from happening? Are there any things that students could do to help in that effort?

Figuratively Speaking — *Activities*

The Moon's the North Wind's Cooky and The Moon Sheep

1. Ask the children to make their own comparisons between the moon and some creature or object. Remind them they may take into account the movement and phases of the moon as well as its physical appearance. Suggest that they make an initial list of at least ten comparisons. Then ask them to choose one or two to develop more fully, perhaps in the form of a poem. To conclude the project, have students illustrate some of the comparisons with drawings, cartoons or prints.

2. Explain to the children that in ancient times people made up stories about the moon, the stars and the planets in order to account for things they didn't understand. Provide selections from Greek and Roman mythology for students to read. They already may be familiar with some of the present-day space programs that were named after the ancient gods who were thought to rule the heavens. Have students research these more recent accomplishments in space.

---

[1] *Nova,* "Life on a Silken Thread," Boston, Mass.

3. Have students discuss a subject, such as the nature of the sun or the movement of the planets, from different historical perspectives. Have pupils choose a particular scientist they wish to portray and research his or her life. A "living" time line could be set up in the form of a debate, with pupils using only the knowledge available in their chosen scientist's time. Copernicus, Newton, Galileo and Werner Von Braun are some scientists that the students might start with. It would be interesting to videotape this discussion and show it to other classes or send it to a local children's T.V. show. If your school does not have the necessary video equipment, perhaps a local news program would be interested in filming it.

4. We have all seen photographs of the earth as seen from outer space. Ask the students to imagine life 100 years from now when we might have a space station on the moon. Have them write a poem about earth from this perspective.

Figuratively Speaking — *Activities*

General Activities

1. Discuss the fact that comparisons can be made in several different ways. Similes are the most common. Similes make use of the words "like" and "as." Ask the children to read the six poems again and pick out the one that makes use of a simile. Have them complete the similes below so they will have a clear idea of how similes can be used.

    1. The puppy wiggled like _____.
    2. The girl's hair was as yellow as _____.
    3. The trees were bent like _____.
    4. The pounding surf sounded like _____.
    5. My sneakers are as beat up as _____.

2. Ask the students to imagine they are political candidates working on plans for their campaigns. Each must come up with a symbol in the form of a logo and a slogan to represent the ideals he or she stands for.

3. Have the students look at the political cartoons in newspapers and magazines to find examples of symbols. Have them identify what each symbol stands for. Which are more effective? Ask them to incorporate the cartoons in a bulletin board display.

4. Have the students set up a "Sign of Our Times" contest. Each student in the school will be allowed to submit one object that symbolizes his or her generation. A requirement might be that each submission be accompanied by an explanation of 25 words or less. Members of the contest committee might pick the best entries or set up a school-wide ballot. The winning ideas might then be included in a time capsule to be opened in a specified number of years.

31

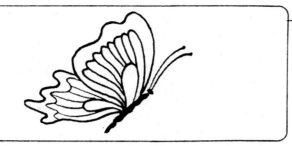

Mood is a feeling or a state of mind; it influences the way we view a situation. Poems have moods of their own and can create certain moods for the reader.

In introducing the concept of mood, it might be helpful to begin with a visual example. Present two pictures dealing with the same subject but conveying different moods. Wyeth's *Her Room* and Van Gogh's *Bedroom at Arles* offer good contrasts. Withhold the names of the paintings until the end of the discussion. Ask the children what type of person might live in each room. What mood does each painting create?

Poets create moods through combinations of words, rhythm and sounds. "Stopping by Woods on a Snowy Evening" by Robert Frost and "Winter" by Richard Hughes give us two totally different feelings about winter. Frost chooses peaceful words that remind us of a gentle snowfall. Hughes describes his scene with short, clipped words that emphasize the paralyzing cold.

"The Deserted House" by Mary Coleridge also creates a feeling of coldness. However, the chill we feel comes not from the elements of nature, but from the absence of any human contact. The mood is not only cold and desolate, but also somewhat foreboding.

In a complete departure from the quiet moods of the previous poems, "Spring" by Karla Kuskin seems to awaken all of our senses. The rhythm is bouncing and lively. The use of verbs such as "swinging," "leaping" and "racing" supports the rhythm and establishes a mood of pure elation.

Winter

Richard Hughes

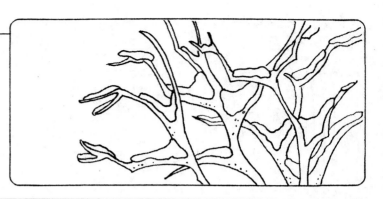

Snow wind-whipt to ice
    Under a hard sun:
Stream-runnels curdled hoar
    Crackle, cannot run.

Robin stark dead on twig,
    Song stiffened in it:
Fluffed feathers may not warm
    Bone-thin linnet:

Big-eyed rabbit, lost,
    Scrabbles the snow,
Searching for long-dead grass
    With frost-bit toe:

Mad-tired on the road
    Old Kelly goes;
Through crookt fingers snuffs the air
    Knife-cold in his nose.

Hunger-weak, snow-dazzled,
    Old Thomas Kelly
Thrusts his bit hands, for warmth
    'Twixt waistcoat and belly.

33

Stopping by Woods on a Snowy Evening

Robert Frost

Whose woods these are I think I know.
His house is in the village though;
He will not see me stopping here
To watch his woods fill up with snow.

My little horse must think it queer
To stop without a farmhouse near
Between the woods and frozen lake
The darkest evening of the year.

He gives his harness bells a shake
To ask if there is some mistake.
The only other sound's the sweep
Of easy wind and downy flake.

The woods are lovely, dark and deep.
But I have promises to keep,
And miles to go before I sleep,
And miles to go before I sleep.

From *The Poetry of Robert Frost* edited by Edward Connery Lathem. Copyright 1923, © 1969 by Holt, Rinehart and Winston. Copyright 1951 by Robert Frost. Reprinted by permission of Holt, Rinehart and Winston, Publishers.

The Deserted House

Mary Coleridge

There's no smoke in the chimney,
    And the rain beats on the floor;
There's no glass in the window,
    There's no wood in the door;
The heather grows behind the house,
    And the sand lies before.

No hand hath trained the ivy,
    The walls are gray and bare;
The boats upon the sea sail by,
    Nor ever tarry there.
No beast of the field comes nigh,
    Nor any bird of the air.

Spring

Karla Kuskin

I'm shouting
I'm singing
I'm swinging through trees
I'm winging skyhigh
With the buzzing black bees.
I'm the sun
I'm the moon
I'm the dew on the rose.
I'm a rabbit
Whose habit
Is twitching his nose.
I'm lively
I'm lovely
I'm kicking my heels
I'm crying "Come dance"
To the fresh water eels.
I'm racing through meadows
Without any coat
I'm a gamboling lamb
I'm a light leaping goat
I'm a bud
I'm a bloom
I'm a dove on the wing.
I'm running on rooftops
And welcoming spring!

Winter and Stopping by Woods on a Snowy Evening
— *Discussion Questions*

1. Both Frost and Hughes describe winter scenes in their poems. Which poem makes you feel the coldest? Why?

2. What words has Frost chosen to describe the wind as compared to those used by Hughes?

3. Have you ever noticed how your moods are affected by types of weather? Explain. Both poems portray a man traveling. What feelings might each of these travelers have toward winter?

4. Look over both poems. Which letter sounds are repeated most frequently in each? How does the choice of sound words affect the mood of each poem?

5. Both poems make reference to being tired. How is this feeling different for each of the travelers?

6. What do you think might have been the promises mentioned at the end of Frost's poem?

The Deserted House — *Discussion Questions*

1. How do we know the house is deserted?

2. How long do you think it has been empty?

3. Where is the house located?

4. What type of person or people might have lived there?

5. Try to imagine what events might have caused the house to become deserted. Compare your ideas to those of others in the class.

6. How does this poem make you feel? If the poet had described just a scene by the sea with no houses at all, would you feel the same way? Why or why not?

Spring — *Discussion Questions*

1. How many verbs or verb forms can you find in the poem?

2. What effect does the choice of verbs have on the mood of this poem?

3. List examples of alliteration.

4. What is the author's point in comparing herself to many different animals and objects?

5. What does the rhythm of the poem remind you of?

6. What is so appealing about spring? What aspects of spring do you find most appealing?

In the Mood! — *Activities*

Spring

1. Have the children write a parody of the poem "Spring," describing something that is unpleasant to them. Their poems might be about the disagreeable aspects of spring or about another subject entirely, such as homework, winter, or a troublesome brother or sister.

In the Mood! — *Activities*

General Activities

1. Play a recording of "Music Box Dancer" by Frank Mills.[1] Have the children describe how it makes them feel. Ask them to reread the poems in this section and choose the one that seems to convey the same mood as the record. Why? How do certain elements of the poem "Spring" (rhythm, rhyme, choice of words, etc.) help to convey a mood of joy and high spirits?

2. The cinquain is an especially good poetic form for expressing moods and feelings. Because it requires no conformity to rhythm or rhyme patterns, students are allowed more freedom to express themselves. Perhaps the class would like to try this format to express moods about subjects of their choice. We have included the formula and an example of this five-line poem below.

   One word for the title
   Two words to describe it
   Three words to show action
   Four words to express a feeling or impression
   One word that repeats or renames the subject

   Example:
   Rain
   Gentle, lovely
   Bouncing, jumping, twirling
   Misty, mad ballet star
   Dancer

3. Write a poem about any kind of house you choose. Draw a picture of the house described in the poem.

4. People, places and objects all around us reflect different moods. As a culmination of the study of moods in poetry, have students set up an "In The Mood" exhibit. This could incorporate hobbies or subjects that are of special interest to the students. The display could be set up in the school lobby, at the town library or at a local shopping mall, so that the students' work could be viewed and enjoyed by the public.

   Have those interested in photography exhibit a series of photographs showing how one subject, such as trees, can depict different moods, or how one mood can be illustrated through a variety of subjects.

   Students interested in drama could do a "live" exhibit of how moods are expressed through costumes, make-up and facial expressions.

   The possibilities for the expression of moods through art are limitless and might consist of original artwork by students or collections of famous paintings. For example, one exhibit might show different moods in art throughout history.

[1] Frank Mills, "Music Box Dancer," Polydor Records.

38

Music can be used as a background for the exhibit, or it can consitutue an individual project.

Students will find they can work together in many areas in which individual projects overlap or complement each other.

The following questions suggest ways in which other subjects can be incorporated into the exhibit.

Science—How do lighting and sound effects create moods?

Science/Social Studies—How does climate affect people's moods?

Social Studies—How do different countries or nationalities reflect different moods in their dress, music, food, houses, etc.? Perhaps students interested in stamp collecting could demonstrate how the mood of a country is reflected in its stamps.

History—How has the mood of your country changed in different eras? How were these changes within one country reflected in different styles of dress, music, art, etc.?

Literature—How do different types of literature such as romance, biography, or gothic novels, reflect different moods? How has the mood of literature changed through history? How does it differ among countries?

Literature/Nature—What different moods are reflected by plants and flowers such as the lily, rose, olive branch or evergreen? What have they come to symbolize and why? What other objects or natural occurrences project certain moods?

A good example of a symbol from nature might be the albatross. What did it first symbolize? Why? How did the connotation change after Coleridge's "Rime of the Ancient Mariner" was written? Discuss the different moods that are evoked by the symbol of an albatross or an "albatross around one's neck."

39

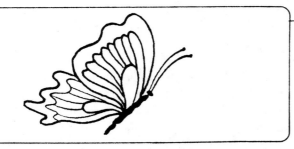

The following selections express various philosophies of life. In the excerpt from "A Psalm of Life," Longfellow tells us we have the power to achieve a kind of immortality through that which we leave behind. He tells us in working toward our goals to be neither discouraged nor self-satisfied but to be constantly striving.

Edgar Lee Masters' character, Fiddler Jones, felt no greater obligation than to remain in harmony with the world around him. He seemed to see himself as an instrument upon which life played a joyous tune.

Henley's poem, "Invictus," depicts a life of constant struggle. The speaker alludes to misfortunes and sorrow that have befallen him, but in spite of these he remains unconquered. He believes the human soul can triumph over any physical obstacles.

The selection from the New Testament points out how transient and corruptible worldly possessions can be. We are told to set our hearts on higher spiritual goals.

Often our outlook on life is shaped by our earliest childhood experiences. Every child at one time has felt that someone else's position in the family is superior to his or her own. Robert P. Tristram Coffin seems to know firsthand the difficulties of growing up as a middle child. The hardships, Coffin tells us, mold the middle child, making him strong, independent, and capable. Coffin sees the middle child as one that will emerge in unlikely situations to demonstrate his talents and strengths.

From **A Psalm of Life**

Henry Wadsworth Longfellow

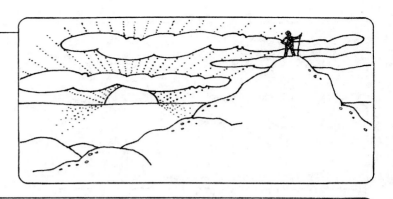

Lives of great men all remind us
    We can make our lives sublime,
And, departing, leave behind us
    Footprints on the sands of time;

Footprints, that perhaps another,
    Sailing o'er life's solemn main,
A forlorn and shipwrecked brother,
    Seeing, shall take heart again.

Let us, then, be up and doing,
    With a heart for any fate;
Still achieving, still pursuing,
    Learn to labor and to wait.

From **the New Testament**

Lay not up for yourselves treasures
upon earth, where moth and rust doth corrupt,
and where thieves break through and steal:

But lay up for yourselves treasures in
heaven, where neither moth nor rust doth corrupt,
and where thieves do not break through nor steal:

For where your treasure is, there will your heart be also.

[Matt. 6:19–21]

The Boy In The Middle

Robert P. Tristram Coffin

Measure the family by the middle boy;
    If he gets on, the family will thrive.
The others should be lively sons, but he
    Has to be more natively alive.

He has to keep his shape and rights between
    The upper and the lower stones of the mill,
The youths and the babies, so he grows good eyes,
    Tough muscles, and a chin all spikes and will.

He learns humility by wearing pants
    Cut from the cloth his brothers have gone through;
His thoughts have plenty chances to mature,
    Since he's the one the rest do talking to.

Big brothers and the baby sit on him
    And mold him right for mankind and the good;
He gets the jobs the others do not want,
    Not splitting but just lugging in the wood.

Too old to baby and too late to love,
    He is the child the parents think of last;
In the true center of the house he sits
    Quiet and sees the household hurtle past.

Likely his ears are just a shade too wide,
    His eyes a blue that is just off a jot;
He looks like neither parent, but himself;
    He is the wistful boy who is forgot.

When wars are to be fought or poems made,
    In times when it seems sure the sky will fall,
It may well turn out the one-horse farms'
    Middle boys are the bumper crop of all.

Reprinted with permission of Macmillan Publishing Co., Inc. from *One Horse Farm* by Robert P.T. Coffin. Copyright 1949 by Robert P. Tristram Coffin, renewed 1977 by R.N. Coffin, R.P.T. Coffin, Jr. and M.A. Westcott.

Invictus

William Ernest Henley

Out of the night that covers me,
    Black as the Pit from pole to pole,
I thank whatever gods may be
    For my unconquerable soul.

In the fell clutch of circumstance
    I have not winced nor cried aloud.
Under the bludgeonings of chance
    My head is bloody, but unbowed.

Beyond this place of wrath and tears
    Looms but the horror of the shade,
And yet the menace of the years
    Finds and shall find me unafraid.

It matters not how strait the gate
    How charged with punishments the scroll,
I am the master of my fate:
    I am the captain of my soul.

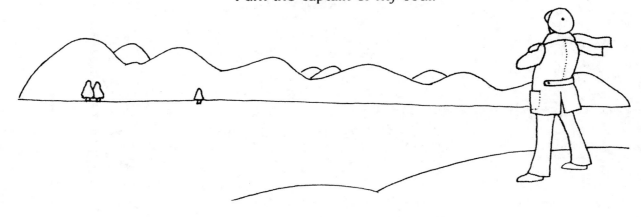

Fiddler Jones

Edgar Lee Masters

The earth keeps some vibration going
There in your heart, and that is you.
And if the people find you can fiddle,
Why, fiddle you must, for all your life.
What do you see, a harvest of clover?
Or meadow to walk through to the river?
The wind's in the corn; you rub your hands
For beeves hereafter ready for market;
Or else you hear the rustle of skirts
Like the girls when dancing at Little Grove.
To Cooney Potter a pillar of dust
Or whirling leaves meant ruinous drouth;
They look to me like Red-Head Sammy
Stepping it off, to "Toor-a-Loor."
How could I till my forty acres
Not to speak of getting more,
With a medley of horns, bassoons and piccolos
Stirred in my brain by crows and robins
And the creak of a wind-mill — only these?
And I never started to plow in my life
That someone did not stop in the road
And take me away to a dance or picnic.
I ended up with forty acres;
I ended up with a broken fiddle—
And a broken laugh, and a thousand memories,
And not a single regret.

"Fiddler Jones" from the *Spoon River Anthology* by Edgar Lee Masters, Macmillan Publishing Co., Inc. Copyright 1914 and 1915 by William Marion Reedy. Copyright 1915, 1916, 1942, and 1944 by Edgar Lee Masters. Reprinted by permission of Ellen C. Masters.

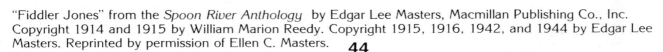

A Psalm of Life — *Discussion Questions*

1. What does the word "sublime" mean?

2. What does Longfellow mean by leaving "footprints on the sands of time"?

3. How does Longfellow's philosophy of life differ from that of Edgar Lee Masters' "Fiddler Jones"?

4. Are the two philosophies similar in any ways? Explain.

5. What type of person might Longfellow be referring to as "A forlorn and shipwrecked brother"?

6. What is the common meaning of the word "wait"? How does this meaning compare with Longfellow's urging to "be up and doing"? Check your dictionary or the *Oxford English Dictionary*.

7. Have you ever been inspired by the life of a great person? Explain.

8. In what ways could you be a good influence on others?

9. What things, other than material possessions, can a person leave behind to benefit later generations?

Matt. 6:19-21 — *Discussion Questions*

1. What treasures do you have that could be stolen or destroyed?

2. What are some of your special talents and personal qualities?

3. Could these be considered treasures? In what ways?

4. Can these things be destroyed or stolen?

5. Some people feel that having few possessions gives them more freedom. Were there ever times when owning something fancy or expensive caused you to worry or miss out on some fun? Explain.

The Boy in the Middle — *Discussion Questions*

1. Find out how grain mills of the 1800s operated. Give a brief explanation of how the grain was ground.

2. What is meant by the phrase, "keep his shape . . . between the upper and lower stones of the mill"?

3. In the poem, who or what were the upper and lower stones?

4. How would both the youths and the babies cause the middle child to develop strong muscles and good eyes?

5. What is humility? Did you ever have to wear clothes that an older brother or sister had outgrown? How did it make you feel?

6. In what different ways do brothers and the babies sit on the middle boy?

7. In the poem, the middle child has the chore of lugging the wood. Who do you suppose gets to split the wood?

8. What is a bumper crop?

9. How might a person be like a bumper crop?

10. Do you think the poet was a middle child? Is there anything in the poem that would suggest this?

45

Invictus — *Discussion Questions*

1. It is clear from the poem that there is a struggle going on. Who or what is the speaker fighting? He mentions one weapon or resource he has to help him in the struggle. What is it?

2. Does the speaker believe he will win the conflict? Support your answer with quotes from the poem.

3. What is the speaker's view of life and the world?

4. Think of someone you have known or read about who had to deal with a personal tragedy. How did it affect him?

5. How important is one's attitude in facing problems?

Fiddler Jones — *Discussion Questions*

1. What sights and sounds in nature remind Fiddler Jones of music and dancing? In what way?

2. What does "beeves" mean?

3. What two different impressions could the wind blowing in the corn make according to this poem?

4. What might the community opinion have been of Fiddler Jones?

5. How much was Fiddler Jones influenced by the people around him?

6. Did Fiddler Jones fulfill a need for the people of the community? Have you ever felt that your talents were needed by a person or a group? How did it make you feel? Can being needed become a burden? Explain.

7. What is meant by a broken laugh?

8. Do you think Fiddler Jones left anything behind for future generations? Explain.

9. Was Fiddler Jones a giving person or a selfish person? Explain.

10. What do you think Fiddler Jones would have done with his life if his neighbors had asked nothing of him?

11. Do people ever do things they don't really want to do? If so, what would motivate them?

In My Opinion — *Activities*

A Psalm of Life

1. Longfellow's "A Psalm of Life" is a good way to introduce a discussion and research project on career choices and goals. Have each student trace an outline of one of his or her feet on a piece of construction paper. Inside he or she will write briefly about his or her career choice and the preparations necessary for a job in that field. These could be displayed on a bulletin board under the title "Footprints in the Sands of Time."

In My Opinion — *Activities*

Fiddler Jones

1. After reading "Fiddler Jones" and the excerpt from "A Psalm of Life," have students set up a series of role-playing episodes. Students could take turns playing the roles of Fiddler Jones and the poet Longfellow. Let the students decide on a setting where these two people might meet to discuss their philosophies.

In My Opinion — *Activities*

Invictus

1. Assign a research project on the life of William Ernest Henley to discover what personal hardships might have prompted the writing of "Invictus."

2. Play a recording of "The Impossible Dream" from *Man of LaMancha*, and have students compare its message to that of "Invictus."

In My Opinion — *Activities*

Boy in the Middle

1. After reading "The Boy in the Middle," encourage members of the class to discuss their own positions in their families. Children should be guided to the realization that each position has its advantages. For example, the eldest child learns responsibility from taking care of younger brothers or sisters. The youngest gains information and help from older children. The only child learns to be independent and sophisticated. Most importantly, the children should not be left with the feeling that the middle child is necessarily unloved.

47

In My Opinion — *Activities*

General Activities

1. Discussion of the poems in this section will give students a basis for examining their own philosophies. Do they approach life with the same seriousness as the speaker in "A Psalm of Life," or with the carefree attitude of "Fiddler Jones"? Do they see life filled with interesting challenges or with unrelenting hardships? Have the students write short essays on their own personal philosophies and goals in life. Tell the children to be as open as possible, since none of the essays will be identified.

   Instruct each child to write a character sketch based on another student's philosophy. Ask them to add personality traits and details of the character's lifestyle. Explain that these are going to be the central characters in a play set at a 35th high school reunion.

   Some characters will be pleased with the way their lives have turned out while others may be bitterly disappointed. Some may have started out with high ideals, as expressed in their philosophies, but circumstances of life and their attitudes may have changed their outlooks.

   Have the class as a whole work out a script giving each character a chance to reflect on his or her life. Perhaps the play could conclude with each character stepping to center stage and reciting several lines of poetry or literature that capsulize his or her final impression of life.

2. Leaders throughout history have left their "footprints on the sands of time." Have the children discuss what personal characteristics make a good leader. Can a person learn to be a leader? What training would be helpful in developing leadership qualities? Have students choose their most admired leader, either from the past or present. What questions would they ask that person if they had the opportunity?

3. Try to arrange to have someone involved with market research visit your class to speak about setting up polls and surveys. A newspaper or broadcasting company might be a good place to inquire. Then have the class set up their own poll on an upcoming election, community problem or school issue. Have them decide how the results of the survey will be published and/or for what purpose it will be used.

4. Good leaders must be able to express their opinions as well as listen to the views of others. Have the class study some of the principles of leadership as set forth by Dale Carnegie and others. Suggested sources for learning how to conduct meetings and deal effectively with other people are listed in the bibliography.

   Ask that each student attend some meeting in the community and note how effectively it was conducted. Was there a valuable exchange of ideas? Have the class discuss what they learned about leadership, both from their reading and from firsthand experience.

   Have the students set up a number of situations that would require holding a meeting, such as gatherings of the school board, service organizations, businesses or social committees.

   Have each student take a short turn at conducting one of the meetings. Certain conflicts among those in attendance could be staged. They should be situations that would demand the leader's immediate attention and leadership skills. Each session should be followed by a brief discussion of how effectively it was handled.

5. Have students research some religion other than their own. Ask that they specifically look for shared beliefs between this religion and their own. Students could share their findings with the class. Conclude with a class discussion on principles that seem to be common to all religions. Do the students feel there are any missing elements that should be a part of all religions?

Chapter 6
I Protest!

Included in this section are several protest poems dealing with child labor, oppression of the poor, and racial prejudice. Protest covers a variety of subjects and can take many forms. A person can protest by striking, boycotting, seceding, petitioning, propagandizing or by using physical force.

Propaganda employs slogans, songs or writing to attack what is viewed as a social ill. Almost every movement depends on propaganda in some form to keep the issue before the public and build sympathy for a cause. However, it is the artist, rather than the propagandist, who makes that protest statement endure beyond the life of a particular movement.

In "The Golf Links," Sarah N. Cleghorn is protesting the use of child labor, a problem that is largely non-existent today. She presents us with a paradox—a ludicrous picture of children shut up in factories while men play games in the open air.

She makes her statement casually, as though it were just a passing observation. Perhaps her offhanded manner is meant to reflect what she saw as society's indifference to this problem. Once we realize exactly what Cleghorn is depicting, we are struck by her ability to make a powerful protest in one deceptively simple sentence.

Don L. Lee's poem "Taxes" protests racial discrimination. He tells us that he pays all the taxes a citizen is normally expected to pay plus the added "black tax." The phrase "black taxes, on everything I do," could be interpreted in different ways, depending on how we define taxes. It is the last two lines that give the poem its impact. The author believes society has charged him extra, both economically and socially, because he is black.

"The Leaden-Eyed" attacks the ageless problems of poverty and hopelessness. Lindsay states that starvation, work, servitude and even death are not the worst horrors to befall mankind. It is, rather, the absence of spiritual and intellectual goals that makes the plight of the poor so tragic and hopeless. The poem builds to a dramatic climax with Lindsay's comparisons between the physical realities that will always be endured and the spritual possibilities that will never be attained.

Taxes

Don L. Lee[1]

Income taxes,
    every year—due
Sales taxes,
    I pay these too.
Luxury taxes,
    maybe—one or two,
Black taxes,
    on everything I do.

The Golf Links Lie So Near the Mill

Sarah N. Cleghorn[2]

The golf links lie so near the mill
    That almost every day
The laboring children can look out
    And see the men at play.

[1] From *Think Black* by Don L. Lee. Reprinted by permission of Broadside/Crummell Press, Highland Park, Michigan.

[2] From *Portraits and Protests* by Sarah N. Cleghorn. All rights reserved. Reprinted by permission of Holt, Rinehart and Winston, Publishers.

The Leaden-Eyed

Vachel Lindsay

Let not young souls be smothered
    out before
They do quaint deeds and fully, flaunt
    their pride.
It is the world's one crime its
    babes grow dull,
Its poor are ox-like, limp and
    leaden-eyed.
Not that they starve, but starve
    so dreamlessly;
Not that they sow, but that they
    seldom reap;
Not that they serve, but have
    no gods to serve;
Not that they die, but that
    they die like sheep.

Reprinted with permission of Macmillan Publishing Co., Inc. from *Collected Poems* by Vachel Lindsay. Copyright 1914 by Macmillan Publishing Co., Inc., renewed 1942 by Elizabeth C. Lindsay.

Golf Links — *Discussion Questions*

1. What are golf links?

2. What are the children in the poem doing?

3. What is unusual about the events described in this poem?

4. Have you ever heard of something being called ironic? What is irony?

Taxes — *Discussion Questions*

1. What different meanings does the word "taxes" have?

2. What is a luxury tax?

3. Do you pay any of these taxes?

4. What is the author telling us in the phrase, "Luxury taxes, maybe—one or two"?

5. What might black taxes be?

6. Look back at your answer for question one and explain which meaning or meanings the author might have intended.

The Leaden-Eyed — *Discussion Questions*

1. Does Vachel Lindsay think the plight of the poor is hopeless or is he appealing for help to relieve their suffering? Defend your answer with specific passages from the poem.

2. Why does he use the phrase "the world's *one* crime" rather than "worst" crime?

3. What does it mean to "die like sheep"?

4. What difference does it make whether a person starves or starves dreamlessly?

5. How can you sow without reaping?

6. Does the style of writing in this poem remind you of any other selection you have read? How would you describe the tone used? Why is it especially effective in this poem?

I Protest — *Activities*

General Activities

1. Have the children look up the word "protest." They will discover that protest means "to state positively; affirm solemnly" and it also means "to make objection to." The word has diverse meanings. Ask them to find out when the word was first used to mean "to make objection to." This should lead children to the *Oxford English Dictionary*.

2. Children will be able to find examples of different forms of protest by looking through the newspaper. They should check news stories and photos for accounts of strikes, demonstrations or rebellions. The editorial page will include protests in the columns, cartoons, and letters to the editor. There may even be ads by special-interest groups protesting existing conditions, proposed laws, etc. Students could cut out articles and display them on a bulletin board under appropriate classifications.

3. Ask the children to think of problems around their school that could be corrected or alleviated in some way. Some suggestions might include the waste of food, fuel or paper; vandalism; littering; excessive noise or an unsafe situation within the school, on the grounds or on school buses. Ask them how the various forms of protest might be applied to each situation. Which ones would be most effective and why?
   Have them pick one or more of the problems to work on individually, in small groups or as a class. Campaigns can include making cartoons, slogans, posters and bumper stickers, presenting speeches or writing letters to the school paper. Students should consider the best times and places to display their work in order to convey their messages most effectively.

4. Have each student choose a biography of some famous protest leader, such as Gandhi, Martin Luther King, Elizabeth Cady Stanton, or Cesar Chavez. Conduct a discussion centered around the events in these people's lives that influenced the courses they were to follow. Were there striking similarities in their backgrounds?

5. Ask the students to research various charitable organizations that raise money to feed and clothe the world's poor. Have them report on the types of services rendered, the numbers and groups of people served, methods of raising money and costs of administration. Which charities seem the most worthwhile? The class might wish to organize a money-raising project and donate the proceeds to the charity of their choice.

6. Students should realize that charity includes serving people as well as donating money to an organization. Ask the class to think of ways that they could personally help people in their community who are in need. Encourage them to follow through with their suggestions. (Church groups, civic organizations or the local social services department might be able to point out areas of real need.)

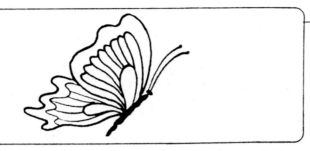

Chapter 7
Tickle My Fancy

There is no set form for a humorous poem. It may be a simple rhyme or a parody of a lofty epic. It might employ satire and irony or rely on exaggeration and nonsense. Perhaps it compels us to laugh out loud or merely smile to ourselves.

While reading the funny and fanciful poems in this section, students will discover ways in which poets use various elements of humor, along with different verse forms and rhythm patterns, to make us laugh, smile or reflect wryly on life. Most importantly, students should have fun with these poems.

The first selection, "Elegy on the Death of a Mad Dog," by Oliver Goldsmith, is a parody of a more serious type of poem. An elegy traditionally praised some worthy person and lamented his death. That Goldsmith chose to compose his poem for a dog—and a mad one at that—sets the humorous tone right in the title.

He paints a satiric portrait of the citizen of Islington, who seems so pious to the sympathetic townspeople. Through the use of puns, Goldsmith points out the difference between the man's public appearance and his private practices. The poem ends with an ironic twist that holds the man up to the ultimate ridicule.

"I Protest" would seem, from its title, to be a poem of high emotion and conviction. However, we find that the tone is one of mock seriousness, as in Goldsmith's "Elegy." It purports to be a protest against the bungling, or perhaps trickery, of elves entrusted with the delivery to us of our rightful share of good luck. At the conclusion of this playful tirade, though, the poet admits to being as capricious as those "mischievous imps."

In "Chang McTang McQuarter Cat," John Ciardi expresses the fanciful notion that a cat's physical and psychological make-up can be expressed in exact fractions. We know it is impossible to compartmentalize the personality of a cat, but at the end of the poem we realize what a truly accurate description we have been given. Ciaridi has not only depicted his cat, but all cats. He states, "Chang McTang belongs to ME," but we are left wondering to what extent such a multifaceted, independent cat can be possessed.

The ballad "Brian O'Linn" makes us laugh because of its outrageous exaggerations. However, it is the resemblance of Brian to certain imaginative, if rather eccentric, people we have known that reinforces the poem's humor. We admire the ingenuity and optimism of Brian O'Linn but are amused by the outcome of his inventions and substitutions.

The section concludes with several limericks. Almost everyone is familiar with the form and rhyme pattern of the limerick and may even be able to quote one or two favorites. Edward Lear is, perhaps, the most famous writer of limericks, having been one of the first to popularize this verse form. Most of his rhymes depend on nonsense for their humor.

The two more recent limericks use a play on words, exaggeration and satire to put their humor on a more sophisticated level.

Brian O'Linn

Anonymous

Brian O'Linn was a gentleman born,
His hair it was long and his beard unshorn,
His teeth were out and his eyes far in—
"I'm a wonderful beauty," says Brian O'Linn!

Brian O'Linn was hard up for a coat,
He borrowed the skin of a neighboring goat,
He buckled the horns right under his chin—
"They'll answer for pistols," says Brian O'Linn!

Brian O'Linn had no britches to wear,
He got him a sheepskin to make him a pair,
With the fleshy side out and the wooly side in—
"They are pleasant and cool," says Brian O'Linn!

Brian O'Linn had no hat to his head,
He stuck on a pot that was under the shed,
He murdered a cod for the sake of his fin—
"'T will pass for a feather," says Brian O'Linn!

Brian O'Linn had no shirt to his back,
He went to a neighbor and borrowed a sack,
He puckered a meal-bag under his chin—
"They'll take it for ruffles," says Brian O'Linn!

Brian O'Linn had no shoes at all,
He bought an old pair at a cobbler's stall,
The uppers were broke and the soles were thin—
"They'll do me for dancing," says Brian O'Linn!!

Brian O'Linn had no watch for to wear,
He bought a fine turnip and scooped it out fair,
He slipped a live cricket right under the skin—
"They'll think it is ticking," says Brian O'Linn.

Brian O'Linn was in want of a broach,
He stuck a brass pin in a big cockroach,
The breast of his shirt he fixed it straight in—
"They'll think it's a diamond," says Brian O'Linn!!

Brian O'Linn went a-courting one night,
He set both the mother and daughter to fight—
"Stop! Stop!" he exclaimed, "if you have but the tin,
I'll marry you both," says Brian O'Linn!

Brian O'Linn went to bring his wife home,
He had but one horse that was all skin and bone—
"I'll put her behind me as neat as a pin,
And her mother before me," says Brian O'Linn!

Brian O'Linn and his wife and wife's mother,
They all crossed over the bridge together,
The bridge broke down and they all tumbled in—
"We'll go home by water," says Brian O'Linn!

"Brian O'Linn" from *1000 Years of Irish Poetry,* Kathleen Hoagland, Ed. Reprinted by permission of The Devin-Adair Company; Old Greenwich, Conn. Copyright 1947 by the Devin-Adair Company; renewed 1975.

Elegy on the Death of a Mad Dog

Oliver Goldsmith

Good people all, of every sort,
    Give ear unto my song;
And if you find it wondrous short,—
    It cannot hold you long.

In Islington there was a man,
    Of whom the world might say,
That still a godly race he ran—
    Whene'er he went to pray.

A kind and gentle heart he had,
    To comfort friends and foes;
The naked every day he clad—
    When he put on his clothes.

And in that town a dog was found,
    As many dogs there be,
Both mongrel, puppy, whelp, and hound,
    And curs of low degree.

This dog and man at first were friends;
    But when a pique began,
The dog, to gain some private ends,
    Went mad, and bit the man.

Around from all the neighboring streets,
    The wondering neighbors ran,
And swore the dog had lost his wits,
    To bite so good a man.

The wound it seemed both sore and sad
    To every Christian eye;
And while they swore the dog was mad,
    They swore the man would die.

But soon a wonder came to light,
    That showed the rogues they lied;
The man recovered of the bite,
    The dog it was that died.

Chang McTang McQuarter Cat

John Ciardi

Chang McTang McQuarter Cat
Is one part this and one part that.
One part is yowl, one part is purr.
One part is scratch, one part is fur.
One part, maybe even two,
Is how he sits and stares right through
You and you and you and you.
And when you feel my Chang-Cat stare
You wonder if you're really there.

Chang McTang McQuarter Cat
Is one part this and ten parts that.
He's one part saint, and two parts sin.
One part yawn, and three parts grin,
One part sleepy, four parts lightning,
One part cuddly, five parts fright'ning.
One part snarl, and six parts play.
One part is how he goes away
Inside himself, somewhere miles back

Behind his eyes, somewhere as black
And green and yellow as the night
A jungle makes in full moonlight.

Chang McTang McQuarter Cat
Is one part this and twenty that.

One part is statue, one part tricks—
(One part, or six, or thirty-six.)

One part (or twelve, or sixty-three)
Is—Chang McTang belongs to ME!

Don't ask, "How many parts is that?"
Addition's nothing to a cat.

If you knew Chang, then you'd know this:
He's one part everything there is.

I Protest!

Donna E. Keene

I protest! I protest!
Wake the townsmen from their rest!
Miserable deed, heinous crime,
I've been robbed of what was mine!
A little clover, four leaves round,
Last summer in the fields I found.
I put in my order; it's been a year.
My four wishes should now be here.
Leave it to elves! What a mess!
Delivered *my* luck to the wrong address!
Those mischievous imps! Horrible luck!
Ooh, a pox on their little delivery truck!
I'd kick every toadstool; I'd hang every elf . . .
If only I weren't one myself!

Three Limericks

A ROCKET explorer named Fite
Once traveled much faster than light.
    He set out one day,
    In a relative way,
And returned on the previous night.

——*Anonymous*

There was an Old Man of Cape Horn,
Who wished he had never been born,
So he sat on a Chair till he died of despair,
That dolorous Man of Cape Horn.

——*Edward Lear*

To manage to keep up a BRAIN
Is no easy job, it is plain.
    That's why a great many
    Don't ever use any,
Thus avoiding the care and the strain.

——*Anonymous*

Elegy on the Death of a Mad Dog — *Discussion Questions*

1. What are we told about the amount of time that the man of Islington spent in prayer?

2. Give two possible interpretations of the phrase, "a godly race he ran." Do you think the citizen was a truly righteous man? Explain why or why not.

3. How is the reader at first led to believe that the citizen was concerned with helping the needy? Who, in fact, was he interested in clothing? Explain.

4. Pick out five words used in the poem to describe dogs. Explain their different shades of meaning.

5. What is a "pique"?

6. What does the death of the dog say about the nature of the man from Islington? How is it insulting to his character?

Brian O'Linn — *Discussion Questions*

1. What type of person is Brian O'Linn?

2. What other characters in stories or poems that you have read would get along well with Brian O'Linn?

3. Would you enjoy having him for your friend? Why or why not?

4. Would you want him to take care of your pet while you were away for a week? Explain.

5. What type of problem might Brian O'Linn be able to help you with?

6. Do you think he was inventive or foolish? Explain.

7. We may laugh at Brian O'Linn, but we've all had to think of substitutes for things that weren't available. Give as many examples as you can.

8. Have you ever heard the expression, "Necessity is the mother of invention"? What does this mean? What innovations did the early settlers or pioneers make?

Chang McTang McQuarter Cat — *Discussion Questions*

1. What point do you think the author was making with the repetition of words in line seven?

2. How can a cat appear to be "one part saint, and two parts sin" at the same time?

3. What part of a cat is like lightning?

4. How can a cat be "fright'ning"?

5. What do you think lines 17-21 refer to?

6. Do you think the author is fond of Chang? Explain why or why not.

7. Are there any characteristics of a cat that Ciardi left out? Explain.

I Protest — *Discussion Questions*

1. What is the speaker upset about?

2. Do you think people are either lucky or unlucky?

3. If you had four wishes what would they be?

4. Do people sometimes tell you that you are lucky when you have actually worked hard for something? How does it make you feel?

5. At the end of the poem the speaker tempers her angry feelings with an admission. What does the speaker say about herself? Do you think people tend to pick out faults in others that they have themselves? Why might this be so?

6. Read again the poem "A Dream Deferred" and compare its mood with that of "I Protest."

Tickle My Fancy — *Activities*

Elegy on the Death of a Mad Dog

1. Have each student write an elegy for the "demise" of some inanimate object they especially liked, such as a comfortable article of clothing, a balloon, a teddy bear, a blanket, etc. The elegies should be humorous but do not have to be written in verse.

Tickle My Fancy — *Activities*

I Protest

1. The author of "I Protest" really does seem to believe in elves; at least she would *like* to believe that they exist and that she is a part of their wonderful, fanciful world. Discuss some of the fantasies that your students wish would come true. What would happen if they did? Ask them to write stories centered around the realization of some fantasy. It might be a place, a person or an imaginary creature, such as the unicorn. Students might enjoy looking through the delightful book *Gnomes*[1] by Rien Poortvliet and Wil Huygen before attempting their own stories.

Tickle My Fancy — *Activities*

Limericks

1. Try composing limericks as a group. Have each student write a first line that would be suitable for a limerick. Put all the first lines into a container. Have one student draw a line other than his or her own. He or she must supply the second line of the limerick. Then have him or her choose a student to contribute the third line, and so on until the poem is finished. Begin with a new line and start a new limerick, giving each student a chance to contribute. The limericks may be written down for the class to keep.

[1] Rien Poortvliet and Wil Huygen, *Gnomes*, Peacock Press/Bantam Books.

Tickle My Fancy — *Activities*

Chang McTang McQuarter Cat

1. John Ciardi says in "Chang McTang McQuarter Cat" that, "Addition's nothing to a cat." It really is important to us, though. Ask the children how many "parts" Chang McTang McQuarter Cat has. Explain that they are to count only the real qualities mentioned, not the "this and thats." Use only the first number mentioned. For instance, in line five the figure is one; disregard the "maybe even two." Now, when the class has agreed on a final number of parts (we come up with 35) they can do some work with fractions. They'll be surprised at how much fun it is this way!
   1. What part of Chang is saint? (1/35)
   2. What part is sin? (2/35)
   3. What fraction describes the part of Chang that is fright'ning? (1/7)
   4. Together, the parts that are grin and lightning make up what fractional part of Chang? (1/5)
   5. Add the parts that are yawn, sleepy, cuddly, fright'ning, snarl and play. What fractional part of Chang do they make all together? (3/7)
   6. Take the total number of parts, minus the number that is sin, and divide by the number that is grin. Answer? 11. Etc., etc., etc.

2. On slips of paper, write out all the qualities that make up Chang McTang McQuarter Cat. Perhaps you'll want to make two or three copies of each so that each student can draw several slips. When each student has drawn several different qualities of Chang, have them draw a picture of the cat, illustrating those traits.

   Remembering that Ciardi's last line tells us his cat is "one part of everything there is," some students might prefer to make a collage, using different pictures from magazines or various materials such as fabrics, buttons, wrapping paper or even bark. Use these to fill in a cat outline or in any other form the student chooses.

Tickle My Fancy — *Activities*

Brian O'Linn

1. The teacher could bring in odds and ends such as buttons, yarn, elastics, feather dusters, a sieve, old sacks, plastic bottles with spray tops or any interesting discarded objects. Ask the children to make something using these materials in different ways. The invention can be useful or fanciful.

2. Have the children make a drawing or life-size model of Brian O'Linn. They will have to be innovative in outfitting him.

3. Brian O'Linn was an inventor of sorts. Do you think he would be able to come up with a useful invention? How do you think Brian O'Linn might cope with the energy crisis? Make up some posters with captions such as "Save Water, Don't Bathe, Says Brian O'Linn." Other areas where conservation is needed could include heat, transportation, lights, etc.

4. Sometimes a remarkable invention can come out of what might seem to be a foolish idea. The children could look up information on Robert Fulton, Thomas Edison or Alexander Graham Bell. It would be good for the children to realize that successful inventors often go through difficult and trying times in their lives. It takes great courage to cope with personal doubt and public criticism. Sometimes it takes time to see the value or importance of an idea or invention.

Bibliography

The following is a list of books, poems and transcripts that students should find interesting and informative.

Carroll, Lewis. "Jabberwocky," from *Through the Looking Glass and What Alice Found There* (published in the same volume with *Alice's Adventures in Wonderland*). London: Octopus Books, Ltd., 1978.

Coolidge, Olivia E. *Tom Paine: Revolutionary.* New York: Charles Scribner's Sons, 1969.

Diven, Anne, Ed. *The Scribner Anthology for Young People.* Edgar Bernstein, "Bird in a Thorn Tree"; Chris Jones (interviewer), "David Silverman: Young Animator"; Robert Epstein, "Arthur the Author: The Getting Started Problem." New York: Charles Scribner's Sons, 1976.

Eaton, Jeanette. *Gandhi: Fighter Without a Sword.* New York: William Morrow Co., 1950.

Engels, Friedrich. *The Condition of the Working Class in England.* Stanford, Calif.: Stanford University Press, 1968.

Freeman, Mae Blacker. *The Story of Albert Einstein.* New York: Random House, 1958.

Garbedian, H. Gordon. *Thomas Alva Edison.* New York: Julian Messner, Inc., 1947 and 1962.

Jansson, Tove. "The Cat," in *The Summer Book.* New York: Pantheon Books, 1974.

Laird, Donald L., and Eleanor C. Laird. *The Technique of Handling People.* New York: McGraw Hill Book Company, Inc., 1943.

Markham, Edwin. "The Man With the Hoe," from *The Man With the Hoe and Other Poems.* New York: Doubleday, 1917.

Meltzer, Milton. *Langston Hughes: A Biography.* New York: Thomas Y. Crowell Co., 1968.

Nova (public-television series). "Life on a Silken Thread" episode. For transcript, write to Nova, P.O. Box 1000, Boston, Mass., 02118. Cost is $3 per transcript.

Petry, Ann. *Harriet Tubman: Conductor on the Underground Railroad.* New York: Thomas Y. Crowell Company, 1955.

Poortvliet, Rien, and Wil Huygen. *Gnomes.* New York: Peacock Press/Bantam Books, 1977.

Reader, W.J. *Victorian England.* New York: G.P. Putnam's Sons, 1974.

Schultz, Pearle, and Harry Schultz. *Isaac Newton: Scientific Genius.* Champaign, Ill.: Garrard Publishing Co., 1972.

Seuss, Dr. *The Lorax.* New York: Random House, 1971.

Shepard, David W., and Paul H. Cashman. *A Handbook for Beginning Debaters.* Minneapolis, Minn.: Burgess Publishing Company, 1966.

Sutherland, Sidney S. *When You Preside.* Danville, Ill.: The Interstate Printers & Publishers, Inc., 1969.

Time-Life Books. *The World's Great Religions: A* Life *Special Edition For Young Readers.* Alexandria, Va.: Time-Life Books, 1958.

Time-Life Television. *Connections.* An excellent television series on inventions. For information on their educational material, write Connections, Box X002, La Jolla, Calif., 92093.

Wilson, Ellen. *Robert Frost: Boy With Promises to Keep.* Indianapolis, Ind.: Bobbs-Merril Co., Inc., 1967.

Wyler, Rose, and Gerald Ames. *The New Golden Book of Astronomy: An Introduction to the Wonders of Space.* New York: Golden Press (Simon & Schuster), 1955.